Winning Chili Recipes

Bonnie Scott

BONNIE SCOTT

Copyright: Bonnie Scott

ISBN: 9781687348333

All rights reserved. No part of this publication may be reproduced, stored in retrieval system, copied in any form or by any means, electronic, mechanical, photocopying, recording or otherwise transmitted without written permission from the publisher. You must not circulate this book in any format.

TABLE OF CONTENTS

CHILI INTRO   7

JALAPEÑO PEPPERS AND SERRANO PEPPERS   9

BEANS OR NO BEANS   10

CHILI POWDER   12

MAKE YOUR OWN CHILI BEANS   14

SUBSTITUTE FRESH FOR CANNED TOMATOES   16

HEARTY HOME-STYLE CHILI   17
BULL RIDER'S CHILI   18
COWBOY CHILI   20
LOVE THAT CHILI   22
BUSY DAY BAKED CHILI   23
SPICY TAILGATE BACON CHILI   24
SPICY CHILI WITH GREEN CHILIES   26
AWARD WINNING TEXAS CHILI   28
FAMOUS TAILGATE CHILI   30
ORIGINAL TEXAS CHILI   32
QUICK CHILI   34
CHILI CON CARNE   35
CHAMPION CHILI   36
GRILLED STEAK CHILI   38
ITALIAN-STYLE CHILI   40
MEGA CHILI   42

CHILI WITH LIMAS	43
MINNESOTA CHILI	44
LOW CALORIE CHILI	45
MEXICALI CHILI	46
SLOW-COOKED CHILI	48
ALOHA CHILI	49
OLD-FASHIONED STEAK CHILI	50
QUICK MICROWAVE CHILI	51

SECRET INGREDIENTS FOR CHILI   53

TURKEY CHILI   54

CHILI WITH LOTS OF VEGETABLES	54
TURKEY CHILI (LOW CALORIE)	56
CATHOLIC CHARITIES CHILI	57
TERRIFIC TURKEY CHILI	58
SPICY SPANISH-STYLE CHILI	59

GARNISHES FOR CHILI - CHILI TOPPINGS - CHILI BAR! 60

CHICKEN CHILI (WHITE CHILI)   62

SOUTHWEST WHITE CHILI	62
WHITE BEAN CHILI	64
SPICY CHICKEN CHILI	66
SHOEPEG CHILI	68
CREAMY WHITE SLOW-COOKER CHILI	70

MEXICAN CHICKEN AND BARLEY CHILI	71
CHICKEN BREAST CHILI	72

VEGETABLE CHILI — 74

VERY VEGETABLE CHILI	74
EASY VEGETABLE CHILI	76
SPICY VEGETARIAN CHILI	78
CHUNKY VEGETABLE CHILI	80
VEGGIE CHILI	81

HEALTHY SUBSTITUTIONS FOR CANNED SOUP — 83

HOMEMADE BEEF STOCK OR BROTH	84
HOMEMADE CHICKEN STOCK OR BROTH	86

BONNIE SCOTT

Chili Intro

Chili. Just the thought of that warm, spicy dish conjures up memories of cook-offs at annual family reunions or a big pot of chili on cold nights with family gathered around.

Everyone has their own idea of what goes into creating the perfect pot of chili. Some like it hot, others – not so much. Some purists scorn the thought of beans in chili while others praise the addition of the humble kidney or pinto bean.

Whatever you prefer, you're sure to find the perfect recipe to satisfy your chili craving in this book. There are recipes with beans or without and varieties that feature beef, chicken, turkey or just vegetables. The number of variations you'll find in these recipes is amazing.

When it comes to heat, chili recipes range from timid to OH MY GOSH! The Scoville Scale is included, so you can get an idea of the difference in temperature between peppers. Add a little or add a lot – it's all up to you and your taste buds!

It's fun to just browse through these chili recipes. You'll be surprised to see some ingredients listed. Maple syrup, French onion soup and baker's chocolate are just a few on the 'List of 36 Secret Ingredients' that will make cooking a pot of chili an unending quest for the perfect chili recipe.

Scoville Scale

Pepper types	Scoville heat units
Carolina Reaper	1,400,000 - 2,200,000
Trinidad Scorpion	1,200,000 - 2,000,000
Ghost Pepper	855,000 - 1,041,427
Chocolate Habanero	425,000 - 577,000
Red Savina Habanero	350,000 - 577,000
Fatali	125,000 - 325,000
Habanero	100,000 - 350,000
Scotch Sonnet	100,000 - 350,000
Thai Pepper	50,000 - 100,000
Cayenne Pepper	30,000 - 50,000
Tabasco Pepper	30,000 - 50,000
Serrano Pepper	10,000 - 23,000
Hungarian	5,000 - 10,000
Jalapeno	2,500 - 8,000
Poblano	1,000 - 1,500
Anaheim	500 - 2,500
Pepperoncini	100 - 500
Bell Pepper	0

Jalapeño Peppers and Serrano Peppers

Some of the chili recipes call for jalapeño peppers or serrano peppers. Serrano peppers are usually green in color like the jalapeño. The heat of the serrano pepper is one step up from the jalapeño pepper and it has the same fresh flavor as a jalapeño.

To use peppers in chili, poke 8 or 9 holes in each pepper. Float one or two serrano peppers or jalapeño peppers at the top of the chili while it cooks. Halfway through cooking, remove peppers, squeezing the liquid from the peppers into the pot. (Or just save the pepper juice in case of needing more spicy heat later.)

Using the Scoville Scale (which measures the heat of peppers), jalapeño peppers are rated 2500 to 8000 SHUs (Scoville Heat Units), serrano peppers are rated 10,000 to 23,000 SHUs, and in comparison, habanero peppers are rated 100,000 to 350,000 and ghost peppers are 855,000 to 1,041,427 SHUs. Ouch!

Beans or No Beans

Chili lovers have strong opinions about one ingredient - beans!

Chili recipes raise disputes among chili connoisseurs as to whether chili should or should not contain beans. Some devotees contend that the word chili pertains only to the basic dish, without beans.

Competition chili won't contain beans. (One chili cook-off spokesman said "There are 2,000 kinds of beans. If we allowed beans, it would become a bean competition.")

The way you like your chili - with or without beans - probably depends on where you were raised. Certain regions like their beans and other regions don't.

Voters AGAINST beans in chili say:

If you live in Texas, no beans! No beans in Texas-style chili unless you want to be banned from Texas.

Chili is short for chili con carne, which is Spanish for "chili with meat". No beans!

In Mexico, there are many different types of chili and beans may be served on the side but not in the chili.

Voters FOR beans in chili say:

Yes, beans! Chili originated as a poor man's meal and beans are an inexpensive filler. Beans add flavor, variety and texture to chili, especially if it is eaten alone as a meal.

Beans make the chili last longer, thus making it more cost effective. So I eat beans in my chili.

Beans in Chili - Yes, because it annoys Texans.

Beans or not, it's still chili.

Chili Powder

To cook a pot of chili for your family, chili powder from the grocery store is fine as long as it is fresh. If the chili powder sitting in your cupboard is a few years old, time to get a new one!

You can also make your own chili powder by roasting chiles, grinding the dried chiles into a powder and adding other spices, such as garlic and cumin, to create homemade chili powder.

Here is a list of specialized chili powders and blends commonly used in chili cook-offs. (Can be ordered online if your grocer doesn't carry them.)

Mexene Chili Powder
Chile Blend - Santa Fe Red
San Antonio Red Chili Powder
San Antonio Original Chili Powder
Cowtown Light Chili Powder
Chile Blend - Fort Worth Light
Dixon Medium Hot Chili Powder

Chile Blend - Bo Prewitt
Chile Blend - Colleen Wallace
Chile Blend - New Mexico Light
Texas Red Dog Chili Powder
Champion Chili Powder Blend

Hot Powders

Chile Pepper Temper-Temper
Ingredients: Red and black pepper, jalapeno, habanero

Terlingua Dust
Ingredients: Ground cayenne, jalapeno and habanero peppers, ground chili peppers

And the best chili cooks agree - add a package of Sazon Goya !

Make Your Own Chili Beans

Many chili recipes use canned beans but it's easy to make your own chili beans from dried beans. Use dried pinto or kidney beans, pick through the beans and discard any discolored or shriveled beans. Rinse well. Soak the beans using the overnight soak method or the quick soak or hot soak method:

OVERNIGHT SOAK

Place dry beans in a stockpot and cover with water. (Use 10 cups of water for every pound of beans.) Cover and refrigerate for 8 hours or overnight. Drain beans in a colander. Rinse with cool water.

QUICK SOAK (or HOT SOAK)

In a stockpot, place beans and cover with water. Use 10 cups of water for each pound (2 cups) of dry beans. Bring to a boil; boil for 2 to 3 minutes. Remove from heat, cover and soak for a minimum of 1 hour or up to 4 hours. (The longer the beans soak, the more tender the beans will be. The "hot soak" method would be soaking for up to 4 hours.) Drain beans in a colander. Rinse with cool water.

COOKING BEANS

The beans need to cook for about an hour before adding them to the chili. So return beans to stockpot. To cook beans, place beans and 3 cups of cold water for each cup of beans into stockpot. Bring to a boil; skim off and discard any foam on the surface. Reduce heat, cover and simmer, gently stirring occasionally, until beans are tender but firm. (Add more water if necessary while cooking.) Test a bean for tenderness by mashing it. Most beans will cook in 45 minutes to 2 hours. Drain beans and set aside. Add to chili when required.

1 cup of dried beans = 2 1/2 cups cooked beans

1 lb. of dry beans = about 6 cups of cooked beans

Substitute Fresh Tomatoes for Canned Tomatoes

Many of these recipes use canned tomatoes but it's easy to substitute fresh tomatoes from your garden.

2 cups chopped tomatoes = 1 (14.5 oz.) can diced tomatoes

Chili Recipes

Hearty Home-Style Chili

4 servings

INGREDIENTS

1 1/2 lb. ground round steak
2 tablespoons vegetable or olive oil
1 (10 oz.) can French onion soup
1 tablespoon chili powder
2 teaspoons ground cumin
1/2 teaspoon pepper
1 (14 1/2 oz.) can sliced stewed tomatoes
1 (6 oz.) can tomato paste
1 (8 oz.) can tomato sauce
2 (16 oz. each) cans undrained red kidney beans

PREPARATION

Brown ground round in oil in a stockpot over medium heat, crumbling with a fork until pink color disappears. Mash beef to consistency of rice.

Put French onion soup through blender at high speed until smooth, about 30 seconds, and pour into meat keeping heat at medium low. Stir in all other ingredients. Heat very gently just until piping hot.

Bull Rider's Chili

6 servings

INGREDIENTS

1 teaspoon chicken bouillon granules
1 teaspoon jalapeño powder
1 tablespoon onion powder
3 teaspoons garlic powder
1/2 teaspoon cayenne pepper
1 1/2 teaspoons black pepper
1 tablespoon paprika
6 tablespoons chili powder
2 teaspoons ground cumin
1/2 teaspoon salt
1 package Sazon Goya seasoning
2 lbs. beef chuck tender steak
1 teaspoon vegetable oil
1 tablespoon chili powder
2 teaspoons granulated garlic
1 (8 oz.) can tomato sauce
1 (14.5 oz.) can beef broth*
2 cups water
2 serrano peppers

PREPARATION

In a medium bowl, combine chicken bouillon granules, jalapeño powder, onion powder, garlic powder, cayenne pepper, black pepper, paprika, chili powder, cumin, salt and Sazon Goya seasoning.

Cut beef into 1/2" cubes. In a 3-quart saucepan, brown the beef in oil. Add 1 tablespoon chili powder and 2 teaspoons granulated garlic while browning. Drain fat.

Add to the saucepan: tomato sauce, beef broth and water. Stir in seasonings mixture. Float the serrano peppers (remove peppers when they become soft.) Bring to a boil, reduce heat and simmer for 2 hours, stirring occasionally.

*Homemade Beef Stock or Broth Recipe pg. 84

Cowboy Chili

6 to 8 servings

INGREDIENTS

2 tablespoons vegetable oil
1 lb. ground round beef
1 green bell pepper, seeded and chopped
2 stalks celery
1 large onion
3 cloves garlic, minced
3 1/2 to 4 cups peeled and chopped tomatoes (about 30 oz.)
1 cup tomato sauce
4 cups beef stock*
2 tablespoons chili powder
1 tablespoon ground cumin
2 teaspoons salt
1/2 teaspoon freshly ground black pepper
1/2 teaspoon dried oregano
Dash of hot pepper sauce
1 cup cooked pinto beans

PREPARATION

Heat oil in a large saucepan; sauté meat, bell pepper, celery, onion, and garlic. Cook until vegetables are tender and meat is browned, about 10 minutes.

Add tomatoes, tomato sauce, 3 1/2 cups of the beef stock, chili powder, cumin, salt, pepper, oregano, and hot pepper sauce. Bring chili mixture to a boil, then reduce heat; simmer for 1 1/2 to 2 hours. Add remaining beef stock if chili is too thick. Add pinto beans and continue to simmer for 30 minutes.

*Homemade Beef Stock or Broth Recipe pg. 84

Love That Chili

4 to 6 servings

INGREDIENTS

1 lb. ground chuck
2 medium onions, diced
1 tablespoon vegetable oil
Salt and pepper to taste
1/2 cup red or green bell pepper, chopped
1 (28 oz.) can whole tomatoes
1 (16 oz.) can chili kidney beans or black beans, drained, rinsed
1/4 cup dry sherry (not cooking sherry)
2 tablespoons chili powder
2 tablespoons honey

PREPARATION

In a large skillet, sauté onions in vegetable oil; add ground chuck and cook until browned. Add salt, pepper and bell pepper. Cook 5 minutes, stirring frequently.

Chop tomatoes into small pieces. In a large heavy stockpot, combine tomatoes, beans, sherry, chili powder and honey. Add ground chuck mixture to the tomato mixture. Cook slowly on stove top for approximately 1 hour, stirring occasionally.

Busy Day Baked Chili

4 servings

INGREDIENTS

1 lb. ground beef
1 green bell pepper, chopped
1 (16 oz.) can tomato pieces or tomato juice
1 (16 oz.) can chili beans (pinto, kidney or black beans)
1 teaspoon salt
1 teaspoon chili powder
1/4 teaspoon oregano

PREPARATION

In a large skillet, brown hamburger. Stir in remaining ingredients and place in a 2-quart casserole. Bake at 300 degrees for 2 hours.

Spicy Tailgate Bacon Chili

6 servings

INGREDIENTS

2 lb. ground beef chuck
1 lb. ground Italian sausage
1 tablespoon olive oil
1 cup onion, diced
1/2 cup green bell pepper, chopped
2 large garlic cloves, minced
8 strips bacon, cooked crisp and chopped
2 (28 oz. each) cans diced tomatoes (with juice)
1 (6 oz.) can tomato paste
3 tablespoons chili powder
2 tablespoons pure maple syrup (or use 1 teaspoon granulated sugar)
Salt and pepper to taste

1 tablespoon beef granules
1 tablespoon chicken granules
1/2 cup beer
1 teaspoon ground cumin
1/8 teaspoon cayenne pepper
1/2 teaspoon Louisiana Hot Sauce
1 serrano pepper
2 (15 oz. each) cans chili beans, drained, rinsed
1 (15 oz.) can chili beans in spicy sauce

PREPARATION

In a large stockpot, heat olive oil over medium heat. Add ground beef chuck and Italian sausage; cook until browned. Drain and set aside.

To the stockpot, add onion, bell pepper and garlic; cook until onion and peppers are tender, about 5 minutes. Add bacon, tomatoes, tomato paste, chili powder, maple syrup, salt and pepper; bring to a boil.

Stir in beef and chicken granules, beer, cumin, cayenne pepper and hot sauce. Add cooked meat. Poke 9 holes in the serrano pepper and float pepper on top. Reduce and simmer for 30 minutes to 2 hours, stirring occasionally. Add beans about 30 minutes before serving. Remove serrano pepper and discard.

Spicy Chili with Green Chilies

6 servings

INGREDIENTS

3 lb. ground beef
2 cups chopped celery
1 large onion, chopped
1 (8 oz.) can green chilies, chopped
6 tablespoons chili powder
2 tablespoons minced garlic
1 tablespoon salt
2 tablespoons sugar
2 tablespoons ground cumin
1 tablespoon coriander seeds
2 (1 lb. 12 oz. each) cans whole tomatoes, pureed
1 (1 lb.) can chili beans in sauce (pinto, kidney, red or black beans)
1 cup shredded Cheddar or Monterey Jack cheese

Garnishes:
Chopped green onions
Shredded cheese
Corn chips
Chopped lettuce

PREPARATION

Sauté ground beef in a large saucepan until brown. Add celery and onion; simmer for 5 minutes. Drain fat from the saucepan and discard.

Add chilies, chili powder, garlic, salt, sugar, cumin, coriander seeds, tomatoes, and beans. Bring the mixture to a boil, then reduce heat; simmer for 2 1/2 hours. Add shredded cheese; simmer an additional 30 minutes. Adjust seasonings to taste. Serve with garnishes.

Award Winning Texas Chili

6 servings

INGREDIENTS

(note: the specialized chili powders can be ordered online)

2 lb. 80/20 ground chuck
1 (10.5 oz.) can beef broth*
1 (15 oz.) can tomato sauce
4 drops Louisiana Hot Sauce
1 tablespoon beef granules
1 tablespoon chicken granules
1 tablespoon onion granules
1 tablespoon garlic granules
1 packet Sazon Goya

1 tablespoon San Antonio Original chili powder
3 teaspoons Cowtown Lite chili powder
1 tablespoon Mexene chili powder
1 tablespoon Dixon Medium Hot chili powder
2 teaspoons ground cumin
1/8 teaspoon salt

PREPARATION

In a heavy, large stockpot, over medium heat, brown ground chuck and drain grease. Add remaining ingredients and simmer for 1 hour to 1 1/2 hours, stirring occasionally.

If more liquid is needed, use additional beef broth. If more heat is required, use a few more drops of Hot Sauce.

*Homemade Beef Stock or Broth Recipe pg. 84

Famous Tailgate Chili

6 servings

INGREDIENTS

2 lb. lean ground beef
1/2 onion, chopped
2 cloves garlic, minced
1 teaspoon prepared yellow mustard
1/4 green bell pepper, chopped
1 to 2 jalapeño peppers, chopped (opt.)
1/4 teaspoon black pepper
1/2 teaspoon chili powder
1/4 teaspoon salt
1 (46 oz.) bottle V8 juice
1/4 cup ketchup
1 (26 oz.) can stewed tomatoes
3 shots Tabasco sauce
1 (16 oz.) can pinto beans or hot chili beans (opt.)

PREPARATION

In a large skillet, brown ground beef with onion, garlic and yellow mustard. Drain excess grease.

In a large stockpot, combine ground beef mixture and bell pepper, jalapeño pepper, black pepper, chili powder, salt, V8 juice, ketchup, stewed tomatoes,

Tabasco sauce and beans. Simmer at least 2 hours on low heat.

Original Texas Chili

6 to 8 servings

INGREDIENTS

4 ancho chile peppers (dried poblano peppers)
4 lb. 80/20 ground beef chuck
1/8 lb. suet (beef), sliced thin
4 tablespoons chili powder
2 or 3 cloves garlic, minced
3/4 cup finely chopped onion
1 teaspoon ground cumin
1/2 teaspoon oregano
Salt to taste

PREPARATION

Wash the ancho chiles; remove stems and seeds.

Boil chiles in a little water for 30 minutes. Save the water when finished. (Remove the chile skin with the back of a knife, if desired.)

Puree chiles with a little of their cooking water in a blender. Set aside.

In a large, heavy stockpot or kettle, cook suet over medium heat until a tablespoon of fat is in the bottom of the kettle. Crumble ground beef into hot suet and stir just until beef is dark gray in color – do not brown.

Add chili powder, stir and simmer for 5 minutes. Add garlic, onion, cumin, oregano and salt. Stir in chile puree. Simmer on low for 2 to 3 hours, stirring and adding a small amount of hot water as needed. (Chili will be thick.)

Quick Chili

4 servings

INGREDIENTS

1 1/2 lb. ground beef round
1 teaspoon salt
1 1/2 cup water
1 (16 oz.) can kidney beans
2 to 3 tablespoons chili powder (2 tablespoons for medium heat, 3 for hot)
1/8 teaspoon sugar
1/4 cup chopped onions

PREPARATION

Crumble the ground round into the salted water in a large saucepan. Cook over medium heat until the ground round is cooked through, stirring constantly.

Add beans and chili powder; mix well. (Use 2 tablespoons chili powder for medium heat or 3 tablespoons for hot.) Add sugar. Simmer on medium-low heat until heated through. Top with chopped onions.

Chili Con Carne

4 servings

INGREDIENTS

1/2 cup sliced or diced onion
2 tablespoons butter
1 lb. hamburger
1 (20 oz.) can red kidney beans
2 (10.75 oz. each) cans tomato soup or 1 can tomatoes and 1 can of tomato soup
1 teaspoon salt
2 tablespoons sugar
1 tablespoon chili powder
1 squeeze of lime juice from a lime

PREPARATION

In a large stockpot, over medium heat, cook onion in butter until golden. Add hamburger and cook until brown and crumbly.

Add kidney beans, soup, salt, sugar, chili powder and lime juice. Simmer for 25 to 30 minutes. Cooking longer improves the flavor.

Champion Chili

4 servings

INGREDIENTS

(note: the specialized chili powders can be ordered online)

2 lb. ground beef chuck
1 (8 oz.) can tomato sauce
1/2 (14.5 oz.) can chicken broth*
1 (14.5 oz.) can beef broth*
1 medium Serrano pepper

1st set of spices:
2 tablespoons Cowtown Lite chili powder
1 tablespoon Dixon Medium hot chili powder
2 teaspoons beef bouillon granules
2 teaspoons chicken bouillon granules
2 teaspoons granulated onion
1/4 teaspoon cayenne pepper

2nd set of spices:
2 tablespoons Mexene chili powder
1 tablespoon San Antonio Original chili powder
1 tablespoon ground cumin
2 teaspoons granulated garlic
1 packet Sazon Goya
1/8 teaspoon black pepper
1/8 teaspoon salt
1/8 teaspoon Terlingua Dust

PREPARATION

In a heavy, large stockpot, over medium heat, brown ground chuck and drain grease. Remove ground chuck from pot, set aside.

Clean pot then add tomato sauce, 1/2 can chicken broth, beef broth and float 1 Serrano pepper (poke 6 to 8 holes in Serrano pepper). Bring to a boil; add Cowtown and Dixon chili powders, beef bouillon, chicken bouillon, granulated onion and cayenne pepper; simmer for 10 minutes,stirring occasionally.

Add ground chuck, reduce temperature to low heat, cover and simmer for 30 to 40 minutes. Remove and discard Serrano pepper (squeeze out juices if desired).

Return to a boil and add 2nd set of spices. Reduce to low heat and simmer for 30 to 45 minutes or until chili powders are completely dissolved.

If more liquid is needed, add some of the remaining chicken broth. If more heat is required, use an additional 1/8 teaspoon of cayenne pepper.

*Homemade Beef Stock or Broth Recipe pg. 84
*Homemade Chicken Stock or Broth Recipe pg. 86

Grilled Steak Chili

6 to 8 servings

INGREDIENTS

4 tablespoons minced garlic
3 cups chopped onion
2 tablespoons olive oil
1 (14.5 oz.) can beef broth*
3 (14.5 oz. each) cans Mexican-style diced tomatoes with chilies, undrained
2 (14.5 oz. each) cans crushed tomatoes
1/4 cup chili powder
2 teaspoons dried oregano
2 teaspoons ground cumin
1 teaspoon black pepper
4 lb. ribeye beef steak

PREPARATION

In a large stockpot over low heat, cook garlic and onion in olive oil for 5 minutes. Add beef broth, tomatoes, chili powder, oregano, cumin and pepper. Bring to a boil; reduce heat, cover and simmer for 1 to 2 hours or until thick.

Broil steak about 8 minutes or until just browned on both sides. Let stand for 10 minutes. Cut steak into

1x1/2-inch strips. Add steak to chili; heat 10 to 15 minutes.

*Homemade Beef Stock or Broth Recipe pg. 84

Italian-Style Chili

4 to 6 servings

INGREDIENTS

1 cup dried pinto beans, rinsed
3 cups water
1 (28 oz.) can diced tomatoes
1 tablespoon olive oil
2 large onions, chopped
2 cups red bell peppers, chopped
1/4 cup fresh Italian parsley, chopped
2 cloves garlic, finely chopped
1 1/2 lb. 80/20 ground beef round
1 lb. hot Italian chicken sausage, casing removed
1 tablespoons chili powder
1 tablespoon Italian seasoning
1 teaspoon ground cumin
1 teaspoon salt
1/2 teaspoon black pepper

PREPARATION

In a large stockpot, add beans and enough water to cover beans 2-inches over. Heat over medium heat to boiling; boil for 3 minutes. Remove from heat. Cover; let stand one hour. Drain.

Add 3 cups of water to the beans. Heat to boiling; reduce heat. Cover and simmer 1 1/2 hours over low heat or until beans are tender. Stir in tomatoes.

In a large skillet, heat oil; cook onions and bell pepper in olive oil for 8 minutes or until tender. Add parsley, garlic, beef, chicken sausage, chili powder, Italian seasoning cumin, salt and pepper. Cook until beef and sausage are thoroughly cooked.

Add skillet mixture to bean mixture. Heat to boiling, reduce heat, cover and simmer for 30 minutes.

Mega Chili

20 servings

INGREDIENTS

6 lb. ground beef chuck
1/4 cup vegetable or olive oil
20 large onions, diced
2 bunches celery
4 tablespoons salt
6 (10 1/2 oz. each) cans tomato soup
2 tablespoons chili powder (or to taste)
3 (15 oz. each) cans kidney beans

PREPARATION

Use minimum 12-quart capacity stockpot. Sauté beef in oil until slightly browned. Add diced onions and celery; sauté for about 5 minutes. Drain.

Add salt, tomato soup and chili powder; simmer for 15 minutes over medium-low heat. Add kidney beans including liquid; simmer for 2 to 2 1/2 hours.

Chili with Limas

4 servings

INGREDIENTS

1 lb. ground beef
4 tablespoons vegetable oil
1 teaspoon salt
1/8 teaspoon pepper
2 cups cooked, dried lima beans
1 1/3 cups bean liquid (from lima beans)
1 (10.75 oz.) can tomato soup
1 (20 oz.) can whole kernel corn
2 stalks celery, cut in 3-inch strips
1 green bell pepper
3/4 cup onion, chopped
1 tablespoon chili powder
2 or 3 drops Tabasco sauce

PREPARATION

In a large stockpot, over medium heat, brown meat in oil. Add remaining ingredients. Simmer for 1 hour.

For 2 cups cooked lima beans, soak 1 cup dried beans overnight in water to cover. Add 1 teaspoon salt and simmer until tender. Do not boil.

Minnesota Chili

4 servings

INGREDIENTS

1 lb. ground beef
1 medium onion, chopped (about 3/4 cup)
2 (30 oz. each) cans kidney beans
2 (8 oz. each) cans tomato sauce
2 tablespoons Worcestershire sauce
1 1/2 teaspoons chili powder
Salt and pepper to taste
2 cups water

PREPARATION

In a large stockpot, over medium heat, brown meat. Drain off most of the fat; add onion and simmer about 5 minutes until onion is tender. Add remaining ingredients. Simmer for 1/2 hour.

For spicier chili, add about 8 drops Tabasco sauce.

Low Calorie Chili

1 serving

INGREDIENTS

1 1/2 cups tomato juice
1/2 cup celery
1/2 teaspoon onion flakes
1/8 teaspoon garlic powder
1 teaspoon chili powder
1/2 lb. lean ground beef
1 (14 oz.) can bean sprouts

PREPARATION

Combine tomato juice, celery, onion flakes, garlic powder and chili powder in a large stockpot. Simmer on medium heat until celery is tender and sauce is rather thick.

In a large skillet, cook ground beef until browned. To the stockpot, add ground beef and 1 cup bean sprouts. Continue cooking for 15 more minutes.

Mexicali Chili

8 servings

INGREDIENTS

1/4 cup vegetable oil
2 lb. beef chuck, 1/2 inch cubes
2 cups sliced onion
1 cup green bell peppers, chopped
1 clove garlic, crushed
2 (1 lb. each) cans tomatoes
1 (6 oz.) can tomato paste
2 tablespoons chili powder
3 teaspoons salt
1 tablespoon sugar
1/4 teaspoon pepper
1/8 teaspoon paprika
2 bay leaves
1 teaspoon ground cumin
1 teaspoon basil leaves
Dash cayenne
2 (1 lb. each) cans red beans
Grated cheddar cheese
Fluffy cooked rice

PREPARATION

In a large stockpot, sauté beef cubes. Add all ingredients except beans, rice and cheese. Bring to boil, then simmer on low heat until beef is tender.

Add beans; heat thoroughly. Serve over rice and sprinkle with grated cheese.

Slow-Cooked Chili

8 servings

INGREDIENTS

2 (1 lb. each) cans kidney beans, drained
2 (1 lb. each) cans tomatoes
2 lb. ground beef, browned
2 medium onions, chopped
1 green bell pepper
1 1/2 tablespoons chili powder
1 teaspoon ground cumin
1/2 teaspoon pepper
Salt to taste

PREPARATION

Put ingredients in a slow cooker in the order listed. Stir. Cook on low, covered, for 10 to 12 hours or on high 5 to 6 hours.

Aloha Chili

6 servings

INGREDIENTS

1 1/2 to 2 lb. ostrich or ground beef
1 large onion
1 (15 oz.) can butter beans, drained, rinsed
1 (15 oz.) can pork and beans
1 (20 oz.) can pineapple tidbits
1 cup ketchup
1/4 cup brown sugar
1/4 cup vinegar
2 tablespoons chili powder

PREPARATION

In a large stockpot, over medium heat, brown meat and onion. Add remaining ingredients. Simmer for 30 minutes.

Old-Fashioned Steak Chili

6 to 8 servings

INGREDIENTS

2 lb. suet
3 lb. onions
5 lb. round steak
3 tablespoons chili powder
Salt and pepper
2 (15 oz. cans) chili beans (pinto, kidney or black beans)
8 cups chopped tomatoes (or 4 15 oz. cans diced tomatoes)

PREPARATION

Slice steak into 1 inch strips; set aside.

In a large stockpot, over medium heat, brown suet; add onions until slightly browned. Add steak; cook until medium rare. Remove pieces of suet.

Add chili powder, salt and pepper to taste. Add beans; simmer at least 3 hours, covered. Add tomatoes 1 hour before chili is done.

Quick Microwave Chili

6 servings

INGREDIENTS

2 lb. ground beef
1 cup onion, chopped
1 (20 oz.) can tomatoes
1/2 cup water
1 1/2 tablespoons ground cumin
1/4 teaspoon cayenne
2 (16 oz. each) cans red kidney beans
5 tablespoons chili powder
1 teaspoon garlic powder
Salt and pepper to taste

PREPARATION

Combine ground beef and onion in a 3-quart casserole dish. Cover with plastic wrap and microwave on HIGH for 10 minutes. Stir and drain.

Stir in remaining ingredients; cover with plastic wrap. Simmer in microwave at MEDIUM HIGH for 20 minutes.

Secret Ingredients for Chili

Secret Ingredients

Bacon
Beer
Honey
Maple syrup
Yellow mustard
Cinnamon
Lime juice
Pinch of sugar
Zucchini
Peanut butter
Diced jalapeno
Chipotle pepper
Chorizo sausage
Ancho chilies
Ground elk
Ground venison

Serrano peppers
Italian sausage
Red wine
Fresh kernels of corn
Brewed coffee
Crushed pineapple
Chunks of pancetta
Ro-tel tomatoes
Liquid smoke
Worcestershire sauce
Habanero hot sauce
Cubed chunk steak
Spicy V-8 juice
Coke or Dr. Pepper
Louisiana Hot Sauce
Sazon Goya

Unsweetened baker's chocolate
Unsweetened cocoa powder
Toasted ground espresso beans
Masa Harina corn flour

Turkey Chili

Chili with Lots of Vegetables

4 servings

INGREDIENTS

10 oz. extra lean ground turkey
1 medium onion, diced
4 cloves fresh garlic
1 tablespoon chili powder
1 teaspoon salt
1 teaspoon ground cumin
1/4 teaspoon cayenne pepper
1/2 teaspoon pepper
2 (28 oz. each) cans diced tomatoes
1 (15 oz.) can black beans, drained, rinsed
2 (15 oz. each) cans fat free beef broth*
4 stalks celery, diced
2 green bell peppers, diced
2 medium zucchini, diced
2 medium yellow squash, diced

PREPARATION

Coat a large non-stick skillet with cooking spray; place over medium high heat until hot. Add ground turkey and onions; sauté with fresh garlic for about 5 minutes or until browned.

Transfer browned turkey and onions to a large stockpot; add chili seasoning, diced tomatoes, black beans, beef broth, celery, bell pepper, zucchini and squash. Bring chili to a simmer over medium heat. Continue to simmer for 30 minutes or until vegetables are tender.

*Homemade Beef Stock or Broth Recipe pg. 84

Turkey Chili (Low Calorie)

4 servings

INGREDIENTS

1 lb. ground turkey
2 teaspoons vegetable oil
3/4 cup onions, chopped
3/4 cup green bell peppers, chopped
1 (28 oz.) can Italian tomatoes, chopped
1/2 (15 oz.) can red beans, drained, rinsed
1/2 teaspoon chili powder

PREPARATION

Heat oil in a large skillet. Add the turkey, onions and bell peppers. Cook until turkey is no longer pink.

Add tomatoes, 1/2 can of beans and chili powder to turkey mixture. Bring to a boil, then heat on low until flavors blend – about 15 minutes.

Catholic Charities Chili

4 servings

INGREDIENTS

1 lb. ground turkey
1 small onion, chopped
1/2 tablespoon chili powder
1/2 teaspoon garlic powder
1/2 teaspoon cayenne pepper
1/2 teaspoon black pepper
1 (16 oz.) can diced tomatoes
1 (6 oz.) can tomato paste
1 (16 oz.) can kidney beans, drained, rinsed
2/3 cup water

PREPARATION

In a stockpot, brown meat, add onion and sauté until translucent. Add chili powder, garlic powder, cayenne pepper and black pepper; mix well. Add tomatoes, tomato paste, beans and water. Bring to a boil, then simmer 30 minutes.

Terrific Turkey Chili

4 servings

INGREDIENTS

1 lb. ground turkey
3/4 cup onion, minced
2 tablespoons margarine
3 cups water
1/2 teaspoon garlic powder
1 tablespoon chili powder
1 tablespoon dry parsley flakes
1 teaspoon paprika
2 teaspoons dry mustard
1 (15 1/2 oz.) can red kidney beans, drained
1 (6 oz.) can tomato paste
1/2 cup pearl barley
3/4 cup shredded cheddar cheese

PREPARATION

In a large saucepan, cook turkey and onions in margarine until turkey is browned and no longer pink in color, about 9 minutes. Drain grease. Add remaining ingredients except cheese to turkey mixture and bring to a boil, stirring frequently. Cover, reduce heat and simmer 30 minutes, stirring occasionally. Uncover and simmer 30 minutes, stirring occasionally. Sprinkle 3 tablespoons of cheese over each serving of chili.

Spicy Spanish-Style Chili

4 servings

INGREDIENTS

1 lb. ground turkey
1 (46 oz.) bottle spicy V8 juice
2 (15 oz. each) cans chili beans (pinto, kidney or black beans)
1 large green bell pepper, diced
2 (14.5 oz. each) cans seasoned diced tomatoes
1/2 cup diced onion
1 to 2 cups salsa or Rotel tomatoes
1 bay leaf (remove before serving)
2 to 3 tablespoons chili powder
1 teaspoon ground cumin
1 teaspoon cilantro
1/2 teaspoon garlic powder
1 teaspoon chipotle seasoning

PREPARATION

In a large skillet, brown turkey. In a stockpot, combine remaining ingredients over medium heat. Add browned turkey to stockpot; simmer on low 1 to 2 hours.

Garnishes for Chili - Chili Toppings - Make a Chili Bar!

Lime wedges
Fresh chopped cilantro
Shredded cheese - Monterey Jack or Cheddar cheese
Sliced black olives
Minced white onion or chopped red onions
Diced or sliced avocado
Shredded lettuce
Sour cream
Chopped tomatoes or pico de gallo

Guacamole
Salsa
Crushed tortilla chips
Chopped scallions
Sliced radishes
Homemade cornbread, crumbled
Crushed Fritos
Greek yogurt
Sliced jalapeno chiles
Cooked bacon

Salsa Verde
Chopped hard-boiled eggs
Chow mein noodles
Diced mango or papaya
Pita chips
Tater tots or rice
Oyster crackers
Crushed saltines
Fried egg on bottom

Chicken Chili (White Chili)

Southwest White Chili

4 cups

INGREDIENTS

1 tablespoon olive oil
1 1/2 lb. chicken breast, boneless, skinless (cut into small pieces)
1/4 cup onion, chopped
1 cup chicken broth*
1 (4 oz.) can chopped green chilies
2 tablespoons honey
1 (19 oz.) can cannellini beans, drained, rinsed
2 green onions, sliced
Monterey Jack cheese, shredded

Southwest Spice Mixture:
1 teaspoon ground cumin
1 teaspoon cilantro leaves
1 teaspoon garlic powder
1/2 teaspoon oregano leaves
1/8 teaspoon ground cayenne pepper or to taste

PREPARATION

In a large saucepan or skillet, heat olive oil over medium-high heat. Add chicken and onions; cook 4 to 5 minutes.

Stir in chicken broth, green chilies and Southwest spice mixture; simmer for 15 minutes on low heat. Stir in beans; simmer for 5 minutes on low heat. Serve topped with green onions and garnished with Monterey Jack cheese.

*Homemade Chicken Stock or Broth Recipe pg. 86

White Bean Chili

12 to 16 servings

INGREDIENTS

2 lb. dried large white or Great Northern beans
12 cups chicken broth*
4 cloves of garlic, minced
4 medium onions, chopped
2 tablespoons vegetable oil
4 (4 oz. each) cans chopped green chiles
4 teaspoons ground cumin
1 tablespoon oregano
1/2 teaspoon cloves
1/2 teaspoon cayenne pepper
1 square of unsweetened Baker's chocolate
8 cups chicken breasts, cooked and chopped
6 cups (24 oz.) shredded Monterey Jack cheese

PREPARATION

Soak beans in water to cover in a stockpot overnight; drain. Add chicken broth, garlic and half the onions. Bring to a boil; reduce heat. Simmer for 3 hours or until beans are very soft. Add additional broth if necessary.

Sauté remaining onions in oil in a skillet until tender. Add chiles, cumin, oregano, cloves, pepper and chocolate; mix well. Add onion mixture and chicken to bean mixture. Simmer for 1 hour. Serve topped with shredded Monterey Jack cheese.

*Homemade Chicken Stock or Broth Recipe pg. 86

Spicy Chicken Chili

6 servings

INGREDIENTS

6 tablespoons olive oil
1 large yellow onion, chopped
2 cloves garlic, minced
2 red bell peppers, seeded and diced
4 jalapeño peppers, seeded and minced
3 tablespoons chili powder
1 1/2 teaspoons cumin seeds
1 teaspoon ground coriander
1/8 teaspoon cinnamon
6 whole chicken breasts, skinned, boned and cut into 1" cubes
2 (14.5 oz. each) cans diced tomatoes in juice, chopped
1 (8 oz.) jar ripe olives, sliced
1 cup beer
1/4 cup grated unsweetened chocolate
Salt to taste

PREPARATION

Heat half the olive oil in a stockpot. Add onion and garlic; sauté for 5 minutes. Add bell peppers and jalapeño peppers; sauté for 10 minutes over medium heat. Stir in chili powder, cumin seeds, coriander and cinnamon. Cook for 5 minutes more. Remove from heat and set aside.

In a large skillet, brown chicken in remaining oil. Add chicken, tomatoes with the juice, olives and beer to the stockpot and stir. Simmer over medium heat for 15 minutes. Stir in chocolate and salt to taste.

Shoepeg Chili

8 servings

INGREDIENTS

1 teaspoon cumin seeds
1 teaspoon lemon-pepper
4 boneless, skinless chicken breast halves
1 clove garlic, chopped fine
1 cup chopped onion
2 (8 oz. each) cans shoepeg corn, drained
2 (4 oz. each) cans chopped green chilies, undrained
2 to 3 tablespoons lime juice
1 teaspoon ground cumin
2 (14 oz. each) cans white or Great Northern beans, undrained
2/3 cup tortilla chips
2/3 cup shredded fat-free Monterey Jack cheese
Non-stick cooking spray

PREPARATION

In a large saucepan, combine 2 1/2 cups water with cumin seed and lemon-pepper; bring to a boil over medium-high heat. Add chicken and return to a boil. Reduce heat and simmer 20 to 30 minutes or until chicken is tender and juices are clear. Remove chicken, cut in small pieces.

Remove fat from the top of the broth and return chicken to the broth. Spray a large skillet with cooking spray; add garlic and stir over low heat for 1 minute. (Careful not to burn garlic.) Add to chicken.

Sauté onions in the same skillet; cook until tender. Add onions, corn, green chilies, lime juice and ground cumin to chicken mixture; bring to boil. Add beans; simmer until heated thoroughly, about 45 minutes. To serve, top with crushed chips and cheese, also salsa if desired.

Creamy White Slow-Cooker Chili

4 servings

INGREDIENTS

2 1/2 cups chicken, cooked and chopped
3 (15 oz. each) cans pinto, Great Northern or cannellini beans, drained
1 1/2 cups green bell pepper, chopped
1 cup chopped onion
2 cloves garlic, minced
2 jalapeño peppers, stems removed and chopped
2 teaspoons ground cumin
1/2 teaspoon dried oregano, crushed
1/2 teaspoon salt
3 1/2 cups chicken broth*

PREPARATION

In a slow cooker, combine chicken, beans, bell pepper, onion, garlic, jalapeño peppers, cumin, oregano and salt. Add chicken broth. Cover and cook on high heat for 4 to 5 hours or low heat for 8 to 10 hours.

*Homemade Chicken Stock or Broth Recipe pg. 86

Mexican Chicken and Barley Chili

6 servings

INGREDIENTS

1 clove garlic
1 cup onion, chopped
1 tablespoon vegetable oil
2 cups water
3/4 cup quick barley
1 (16 oz.) can chopped tomatoes
1 (16 oz.) can tomato sauce
1 (14 1/2 oz.) can chicken broth*
1 (11 oz.) can corn (drained)
1 (4 oz.) can green chilies (drained)
1 tablespoon chili powder
1/2 teaspoon ground cumin
3 cups chicken breast, cooked and chopped

PREPARATION

In a stockpot over medium heat, cook garlic and onion in vegetable oil until tender. Add water, barley, tomatoes, tomato sauce, chicken broth, corn, green chilies, chili powder and cumin. Bring to a boil. Reduce heat to low. Simmer, covered, for 10 minutes. Add chicken and continue simmering for 5 to 10 minutes or until chicken is heated and barley is tender.

Homemade Chicken Stock or Broth Recipe pg. 86

BONNIE SCOTT

Chicken Breast Chili

4 to 6 servings

INGREDIENTS

1 cup tomato juice
1 cup raw cracked wheat (bulgur)
2 tablespoons vegetable oil
3 garlic cloves, crushed
1 large onion, chopped
3 carrots, chopped
3 celery stalks, chopped
1 (14 oz.) can Italian plum tomatoes, with juice
2 cups dry pinto beans, cooked
3 cups cooked chicken breast, cubed
1 (4 oz.) can chopped green chilies
1/4 cup chili powder
1 teaspoon dried oregano
2 teaspoons ground cumin
1/8 teaspoon black pepper
1 (12 oz.) bottle beer
Salt to taste

PREPARATION

In a medium saucepan over medium heat, bring tomato juice to a boil. Remove from heat and add cracked wheat. Cover; let stand 15 minutes.

In a large stockpot over medium heat, heat oil. Add garlic and onions and cook until soft. Add carrots, celery, tomatoes with juice. Cover and cook until carrots and celery are tender, about 20 minutes.

Add beans, chicken, green chilies, chili powder, oregano, cumin, black pepper and beer. Simmer for 30 minutes partly covered, stirring occasionally. Season with salt.

Vegetable Chili

Very Vegetable Chili

6 servings

INGREDIENTS

2 large onions, chopped
1 medium green bell pepper, chopped
3 garlic cloves, minced
1 tablespoon vegetable oil
1/2 cup water
2 medium carrots, cut into chunks
2 medium potatoes, peeled and cubed
1 (14 oz.) can fat-free chicken broth*
1 to 2 tablespoons chili powder
2 tablespoons sugar
1 teaspoon ground cumin
3/4 teaspoon dried oregano
1 small zucchini, sliced 1/4 inch thick
2 (28 oz. each) cans crushed tomatoes
1/3 cup ketchup
1 (16 oz.) can kidney beans, drained, rinsed
1 (15 oz.) can garbanzo beans, drained, rinsed
1 (15 1/2 oz.) can black-eyed peas, drained, rinsed

PREPARATION

In a large stockpot, sauté onions, bell pepper and garlic in oil until tender. Add water and carrots; cover and cook over medium-low heat for 5 minutes.

Add potatoes, chicken broth, chili powder, sugar, cumin and oregano; cover and cook for 10 minutes. Add zucchini, tomatoes and ketchup; bring to boil. Reduce heat, cover and simmer for 15 minutes. Stir in beans and black-eyed peas; simmer for 10 to 15 minutes.

*Homemade Chicken Stock or Broth Recipe pg. 86

Easy Vegetable Chili

6 servings

INGREDIENTS

2 medium potatoes
1 medium onion
1 small yellow bell pepper
1 (16 oz.) can garbanzo beans
1 (16 oz.) can kidney beans
1 (28 oz.) can whole tomatoes, undrained
1 (8 oz.) can tomato sauce
1 tablespoon chili powder
1 teaspoon ground cumin
1 medium zucchini

PREPARATION

Scrub potatoes thoroughly but do not peel. Cut into cubes 1/2 inch or larger, Peel and chop onion. Place potatoes and onion in a 4 quart stockpot.

Cut bell pepper in half and remove seeds. Chop into small pieces and add to stockpot. Drain beans in a strainer and rinse with cool water. Add to mixture. Add the tomatoes with their liquid, tomato sauce, chili powder and cumin. Heat to boiling over high heat, breaking up the tomatoes with a fork and stirring occasionally.

Once boiling, reduce heat enough so chili is bubbling gently. Cover and cook for 10 minutes. While chili is cooking, cut zucchini into 1/2 inch slices. Stir into chili. Cover and cook for 5 to 7 minutes, stirring occasionally, until potatoes and zucchini are tender when pierced with a fork.

Spicy Vegetarian Chili

8 servings

INGREDIENTS

1 onion, chopped
1 green bell pepper, chopped
1 red bell pepper, chopped
1 tablespoon vegetable oil
1/2 teaspoon mustard seeds
1 (28 oz.) can chopped tomatoes
1 (15.5 oz.) can pinto beans
1 (15.5 oz.) can kidney beans
2 carrots, peeled and chopped
2 jalapeño peppers, seeded and minced
1/2 can (3 oz.) tomato paste
2 teaspoons chili powder
1 teaspoon ground cumin
1/4 teaspoon unsweetened baking cocoa
1/8 teaspoon ground cinnamon

PREPARATION

In a heavy, large stockpot, heat oil over medium high heat. Cook onion, green and red peppers until soft and golden, about 5 minutes. Add mustard seeds; cook for 1 minute, stirring often.

Rinse and drain pinto beans and kidney beans. To the stockpot, add tomatoes (undrained), pinto beans, kidney beans, carrots, jalapeño, tomato paste, chili powder, cumin, cocoa and cinnamon. Stir well. Reduce heat and simmer, uncovered, for about 40 minutes or until thickened, stirring occasionally.

Chunky Vegetable Chili

8 servings

INGREDIENTS

1 medium onion, chopped
1 medium green bell pepper, chopped
3 garlic cloves, minced
1 tablespoon olive oil
2 (14.5 oz. each) cans Mexican-style stewed tomatoes, undrained
2 1/2 cups water
1 cup uncooked long-grain rice
1 (16 oz.) kidney beans, drained, rinsed
1 (11 oz.) can whole kernel corn, drained
1 (15 oz.) can pinto beans, drained, rinsed
1 to 2 tablespoons chili powder
1 1/2 teaspoons ground cumin

PREPARATION

In a stockpot over medium heat, sauté onion, bell pepper and garlic in oil until tender. Stir in remaining ingredients; bring to a boil. Reduce heat and cover; simmer 20 to 30 minutes or until rice is cooked, stirring occasionally.

Veggie Chili

4 servings

INGREDIENTS

1 onion, chopped
3 cloves garlic, minced
1/2 green bell pepper, chopped
1 tablespoon olive oil
1 (15 oz.) can black beans, drained, rinsed
1 cup frozen corn, thawed
1 (15 oz.) can tomatoes, with juice, chopped
1 tablespoon tomato paste
2 tablespoons green chiles
1 tablespoon chili powder
1 teaspoon ground cumin
Jalapeño peppers, chopped, to taste (optional)
Sourdough bread bowls

PREPARATION

In a stockpot, sauté onion, garlic and bell pepper in oil. Add remaining ingredients. Cook over medium-low heat for 15 to 20 minutes. Serve in sourdough bread bowls.

Healthy Substitutions for Canned Soup

Most busy cooks use shortcuts whenever they can. Those cans of condensed soup and broth save loads of time when dinner has to be ready in a hurry. But by making your own broths and cream soups, you have more control of the amount of sodium and fat in your family's diet.

Plus, the homemade flavor just can't be beat! See the following pages for beef stock or broth recipe and chicken stock or broth recipe.

Homemade Beef Stock or Broth

Classic beef stock begins by slowly roasting the soup bones, a process that will caramelize the bones. Alternatively, you can also caramelize the bones in 1 to 2 tablespoons of vegetable oil over medium-high heat in a large saucepan (in batches) for a few minutes on each side. Using this method is faster, but the hot fat will splatter. After removing the bones from the saucepan, drain most of the excess fat, add a little water, add carrots and onion and cook until browned.

A real bone stock is made with bones and cuts of meat high in collagen, like marrow, feet and knuckles but any bones can be used.

To make homemade beef broth, use the same recipe as for stock but add meat in with the bones or use meaty soup bones such as short ribs or beef shanks and leave the meat on the bones for more flavor. Beef broth and stock are interchangeable in most recipes. Broth is made with more actual meat versus the stripped bones used for beef stock.

6 lbs. beef soup bones
3 large carrots
1 medium onion
2 celery stalks (especially the tops)
1 medium potato
1 large tomato

2 cloves garlic
2 bay leaves
1 teaspoon salt
1/4 teaspoon black pepper
Water

Blanching - This step, to be done before roasting and cooking, removes the impurities from the bones. To blanch, cover the bones with cold water, bring to a boil, and let them cook at an aggressive simmer for 20 minutes before draining and roasting.

Roasting - Wash carrots and chop into 1-inch pieces. Cut onion into chunks. In a shallow roasting pan, place carrots, onion and soup bones. Bake at 450 degrees F. for 30 minutes or until bones are well browned, turning occasionally.

Drain fat. Add 1/2 cup water to roasting pan with soup bones; pour all into a large stock pot.

Wash and roughly chop celery, potato (with peel) and tomato into large pieces. Add celery, potato, tomato, garlic, bay leaves, salt and pepper to stock pot. Pour in just enough cold water to cover, bring to a boil, reduce heat to a simmer, and cover.

Skim any fat and foam from the surface of the water. Simmer for 3 to 5 hours. Strain stock through a fine-mesh sieve into a shallow, wide container, pressing on solids; discard solids. Let the finished broth cool slowly before transferring to refrigerator.

Homemade Chicken Stock or Broth

If making chicken stock for freezing, you may want to simmer the stock for an hour or so longer, making it more concentrated and easier to store. Stock can also be made in a slow cooker.

When making stock, remember the flavor is derived from the bones, not the meat on the bones.

To make homemade chicken broth, use the same recipe as for chicken stock but add meat in with the bones or use meaty bones for more flavor. Chicken broth and stock are interchangeable in most recipes. Broth is made with more actual chicken versus the stripped bones used for chicken stock.

Leftover bones and skin from a chicken carcass
2 celery stalks (especially the tops)
1 medium onion
1 or 2 carrots
1 teaspoon salt
1/4 teaspoon black pepper
1 bay leaf
2 fresh parsley sprigs

Chop celery, onion and carrots into large pieces. Using a large stock pot, add chicken bones, skin, celery, onion and carrots. Cover with cold water. Add salt, pepper, bay leaf and parsley. Bring to a boil; reduce heat to simmer. Simmer, partially covered, for 4 hours or more, using a slotted spoon to remove any foam from the surface.

Remove and discard bones, skin and vegetables. Strain stock through a colander lined with cheesecloth or a clean tea towel, or a fine-meshed sieve. Cool quickly in refrigerator.

Hey, if you loved this book and want to get more freebies and recipes like these, subscribe to the newsletter at:

http://www.BonnieScottAuthor.com/subscribe.html

Also by Bonnie Scott

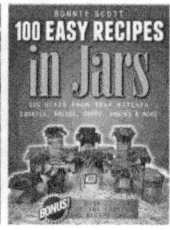

Cookie Indulgence – 150 Easy Cookie Recipes

4 Ingredient Cookbook: 150 Quick Timesaving Recipes

100 Easy Recipes in Jars

Chocolate Bliss: 150 Easy Chocolate Recipes

100 Easy Camping Recipes

View more of my books at my Amazon Author Page - https://www.amazon.com/Bonnie-Scott/e/B008MM40AY

Made in the USA
Monee, IL
23 December 2024